A Guide to Building a Loving Partnership

Actionable Tips to Mastering the Psychology of Relationship

by

Paul E. Kirsch

About the Author

Paul E. Kirsch is a renowned relationship coach, author, and speaker dedicated to helping individuals and couples build strong, healthy, and fulfilling relationships. With over two decades of experience in the field of relationship dynamics and personal development, Paul has become a trusted voice in the realm of self-help and emotional wellness.

Paul's passion for understanding the intricacies of human connection began early in his career as a licensed therapist, where he worked with individuals and couples facing a wide range of relational challenges. His approach combines psychological insights with practical, actionable advice, making complex concepts accessible and applicable to everyday life.

Paul holds a Master's degree in Clinical Psychology and is a certified relationship coach. His extensive background in therapy and coaching has equipped him with a deep understanding of the psychological principles that underpin successful relationships. Over the years, he has developed a unique methodology that emphasizes the importance of communication, empathy, and mutual growth in fostering loving partnerships.

TABLE OF CONTENT

INTRODUCTION

Welcome to "A Guide to Building a Loving Partnership: Actionable Tips to Mastering the Psychology of Relationships."

In the journey of life, few experiences rival the depth and richness of a loving partnership. Relationships form the cornerstone of our emotional well-being and personal growth, Whether with a romantic partner, family member, or close friend. Yet, despite their importance, relationships often present challenges that can leave us feeling confused, frustrated, or disconnected.

This book is your roadmap to navigating those challenges and cultivating a relationship that thrives on mutual understanding, respect, and love. Drawing upon insights from psychology and years of research, we will explore the fundamental aspects of building and sustaining a loving partnership.

Each chapter will delve into a key aspect of relationship dynamics, offering practical advice, actionable tips, and thought-provoking exercises to help you deepen your connection with your partner and create a relationship that brings joy, fulfillment, and meaning to your life.

Whether you're embarking on a new relationship, seeking to strengthen an existing one, or simply curious about the mysteries of human connection, this book is here to guide you every step of the way. Together, let's embark on a journey of discovery, growth, and love as we unravel the complexities of building a loving partnership.

CHAPTER 1

GROWING TOGETHER

In the grand landscape of love, nurturing our bonds is like giving life to a garden. Just as plants need rich soil to grow, our relationships thrive on care and attention. Let's dive into how couples can grow together, adapt to change, and support each other's growth.

Exploring Relationship Growth Dynamics

Think of relationships as ever-changing, just like us. They shift and transform with every shared moment and challenge. Growth is at the core of these changes, molding our connections and strengthening our ties.

The beauty of being together is in the shared experiences—adventures, tough times, and celebrations. These moments aren't just memories; they build intimacy and trust. And when we face obstacles, that's when our bond truly shows its strength. Working through differences and struggles can bring us closer, fostering empathy and a deeper connection.

But growth isn't just about overcoming adversity. Happy times, like reaching goals or simply enjoying each other's company, are just as important. They highlight the good in our relationship, creating a sense of togetherness and thankfulness.

Each person also brings their individuality to the relationship, with unique dreams and challenges. Growing together means cheering each other on, sharing in each other's journeys, and being each other's support system.

To get the dynamics of growth, we need to be okay with change and vulnerability. Open communication, respect, and a commitment to learning are key. When we approach our relationship with curiosity and compassion, it can evolve and blossom beautifully.

Nurturing Our Own and Each Other's Growth

In the tapestry of love, growth isn't just about us as a couple; it's also about our journeys. We need to create a supportive space where each person feels free to chase their dreams and passions while still nurturing the relationship.

It's all about respecting and understanding each other's unique qualities. When we communicate openly and celebrate each other's wins, we create a safe place for personal growth.

Encouraging each other to follow our interests and ambitions is crucial. At the same time, we should also focus on growing together by setting common goals and visions for the future.

Teamwork is magic. Sharing activities and working together on projects can strengthen our connection and foster a sense of shared growth.

In the end, nurturing growth, both individually and together, means being dedicated to continuous learning and self-discovery. It's about building an environment where we feel empowered to grow, both on our own and as a couple, making our relationship richer and more fulfilling.

Embracing Change Together

Life is full of change, and for couples, being able to roll with these changes is vital. Embracing change means seeing it not as a threat but as a chance for growth and new experiences. With an open heart and a willingness to adapt, we can face life's shifts with excitement.

Communication is key when it comes to change. We need to talk about our feelings and support each other through transitions. Staying adaptable helps us tackle the unexpected with creativity and a shared eagerness to learn.

Supporting each other's dreams, even when they're different from our own, is part of embracing change. It's about mutual respect and encouragement.

But embracing change doesn't mean we give up on stability. Having a solid foundation of trust and shared values keeps us anchored during turbulent times.

Ultimately, embracing change is about embracing life together, with all its ups and downs. It's about sharing a journey of growth and transformation, knowing we have each other's backs. By welcoming change as a couple, we build a relationship that's resilient, dynamic, and full of potential for happiness and growth.

CHAPTER 2

THE SELF-ESTEEM FACTOR

Self-worth is often seen as the bedrock of mental well-being and is crucial in influencing how we think, feel, and act, especially in our interactions with others. In this discussion, we're going to delve into how self-worth and the dynamics of our relationships intertwine, and we'll look at how a solid sense of self can lead to stronger bonds, better communication, and more joy in our partnerships.

Let's Talk About Self-Worth and Its Impact on Relationships

At the heart of it, self-worth is about how much we value ourselves. It's about our beliefs concerning our abilities, our deservingness of love, and our overall significance. These beliefs form the foundation of our identity and how we see ourselves. When it comes to romance and friendships, self-worth is a major player, affecting everything from how we chat with our partners to our capacity for trust and openness.

People with a robust sense of self-worth bring a vibe of confidence and stability to their relationships. They're good at voicing their needs, setting healthy boundaries, and keeping their independence within a partnership. On the flip side, those with shaky self-worth might grapple with feelings of not being good enough, which can lead to trouble in expressing themselves, holding their ground, and connecting with their partners.

Tips for Boosting and Preserving a Positive Sense of Self-Worth

Cultivating and keeping up a healthy self-worth is an ongoing process that takes conscious effort and self-examination. Let's explore some ways to nurture a positive view of ourselves, enhance our self-assurance, and strengthen our overall self-worth.

One key method is embracing self-compassion. This means being as kind and understanding to ourselves as we would be to a friend, especially during tough times. By being gentler and more supportive of ourselves, we can grow more accepting and bounce back more easily from setbacks.

Another crucial step is to tackle the negative chatter in our heads and the self-limiting beliefs we might hold. These often stem from past experiences or societal pressures and can lead to a sense of unworthiness. By confronting and reshaping these thoughts, we can adopt more uplifting and confident views of ourselves.

Also, let's not forget about self-care and making our needs and happiness a priority. This can mean doing things we love, setting boundaries, and seeking support when necessary. By focusing on self-care, we feed our inner selves and build a solid base of self-worth that helps us flourish in our relationships.

Encouraging a Supportive and Affirming Partnership

Beyond working on our self-worth, it's also vital to nurture an environment of mutual support and affirmation in our relationships. This is about creating a space where both people feel seen, heard, and respected for who they are.

One approach is to practice active listening and empathy. Hearing out our partner and trying to get where they're coming from without judgment can go a long way. By showing empathy, we create a comforting space where both parties feel understood and appreciated.

It's also important to regularly show gratitude and acknowledge our partner's good traits and what they bring to the table. Whether it's thanking them for their support, recognizing their achievements, or just expressing love often, these gestures can deepen trust, intimacy, and connection.

Nurturing our self-worth is key to having a strong and satisfying relationship. By getting to grips with how self-worth influences our interactions, practicing self-kindness, and encouraging a reciprocal support system with our partner, we can build a partnership based on confidence, trust, and mutual respect. Investing in our growth and our partner's happiness can lead to a bond that allows both people to shine, bringing more joy and closeness into the relationship.

CHAPTER 3

MEANING OF CONFLICT

Conflict is just part of being in any kind of relationship, whether with your sweetheart, family, or pals. It gets a bad rap for causing trouble, but it can actually help relationships grow stronger, get folks to understand each other better, and bring them closer together. In this chat, we're going to dive into what makes conflict tick, how it can mean different things, and how it can end up being a good thing for relationships.

Getting to Know Conflict

Let's face it, conflict pops up because people just naturally bump heads over different stuff. Maybe it's what they believe in, what they want, or how they talk to each other. It's just what happens when two people with their ideas and wishes get together. Sure, conflict can be a bit of a pain and make us feel all kinds of uncomfortable, but it's a normal, healthy part of being close to someone. It's how we tell each other what we need, sort out our differences, and get where the other person is coming from.

Now, don't think conflict is all bad news. Handled the right way, it can make a relationship stronger, with more trust and respect. The trick is to talk things out openly, really listen to each other, and come up with solutions that work for everyone. That way, what could've been a big headache turns into a chance for positive change.

The Ins and Outs of Conflict

Conflict comes in all shapes and sizes and can be sparked by loads of different things in a relationship. Maybe you don't see eye to eye on something important, or someone's expectations aren't being met, or there's some old grudge that's never been sorted out. Outside stress, like job hassles or money worries, can also make things tenser at home.

Getting the hang of what's behind conflict helps you deal with it better. Usually, it follows a pattern where things heat up, everyone has their say, you work through it, and then you make up. By getting to know these stages and how you usually handle conflict, you can get better at spotting what sets you off, how you communicate, and how you can fix things.

Growing and Understanding Through Conflict

Even though conflict might start with getting mad or upset, it's also a golden chance to grow and get to know each other better. If you approach it with an open mind, a caring heart, and a readiness to talk things through, conflict can lead to a deeper bond, a stronger connection, and more respect for each other.

One of the best things about conflict is that it lets both people say what they need and want, clear and straight. Talking honestly and kindly helps you understand where the other person is coming from, which can lead to feeling more empathy, getting each other, and feeling validated in the relationship.

Plus, conflict is a great time to practice key relationship skills like really listening, speaking up for yourself, and solving problems together. By learning to handle disagreements with patience, empathy, and respect, you can boost your communication skills and build a relationship that's full of trust and closeness.

So, conflict doesn't have to be bad news for a relationship. With the right attitude and a willingness to talk things out, it can be a way to grow, understand each other better, and get closer. By figuring out what conflict means and how it works, couples can turn those tough times into chances for more connection, respect, and positive vibes.

Chatting Through Conflict

When couples hit a rough patch, how they talk it out can make or break their connection. Good communication during these times is key to understanding each other's point of view, sharing emotions in a good way, and coming up with solutions that make everyone happy. Let's look at some top tips for talking through the tough stuff with empathy, respect, and understanding.

Active Listening

Active listening is a must-have skill for chatting through conflict. It means tuning in to what your other half is saying, without cutting them off or zoning out. Give them your full attention, make eye contact, and keep those interruptions on hold. Instead of thinking up your comeback while they're talking, focus on getting what they're saying. Repeating back what you've heard in your own words can show you're listening and encourage more sharing.

Spilling the Beans on Feelings

When you're in the middle of a spat, it's super important for both of you to share your feelings and needs without pointing fingers or getting defensive. Stick to "I" statements that talk about your own feelings, like "I feel left out when we don't chat about our day." This way, you're not blaming anyone, and you're making it safe to have a real, open conversation.

Understanding with Empathy

Getting where your partner's coming from, even if you don't agree, can go a long way. Show some empathy by recognizing their emotions and showing that you get why they feel that way. Something like, "I see why this upset you, and I get why it matters to you," can make them feel heard and supported.

Ditching the Défense

Getting defensive or throwing out criticisms can just turn up the heat on a disagreement. Try to stay open, curious, and understanding instead. Skip the blame game, and focus on getting their viewpoint and finding common ground. Remember, conflict is a chance to grow closer, not to drive a wedge between you.

Working Together for Solutions

In the end, chatting through conflict is all about finding answers that make both sides happy. This means being ready to work together, thinking up creative fixes, and looking at things from new angles. Instead of seeing it as a battle where someone has to win, treat it as a team effort to solve a problem where everyone's voice matters.

Wrapping It Up

Good communication during conflict keeps trust, closeness, and respect alive in a relationship. By really listening, sharing feelings, showing empathy, steering clear of defensiveness, and looking for solutions, couples can get through the rough spots with grace and understanding, making their bond even stronger.

Making Peace with Conflict

Conflict is just part of the deal in relationships, but it's not all doom and gloom. It can be a chance to grow, get each other, and feel even more connected. Here's how to make the most of those tricky times and come out stronger on the other side.

Embracing Differences

First things first, getting past conflict means accepting that you're both different. Everyone has their own way of seeing things, and that's okay. When you realize that these differences are normal, you can start to tackle conflict with more empathy, curiosity, and a real desire to understand where the other person is coming from.

Safe Space

For conflict to get resolved in a good way, you need a space where everyone feels safe and respected. Set some rules for how you'll talk to each other, like no name-calling or shouting, and agree to treat each other kindly, no matter what. This safe zone lets you both speak freely and honestly, which is super important for working things out.

Listening and Understanding

To solve conflict, you've got to listen and try to understand where the other person is coming from. Pay full attention, make eye contact, and don't interrupt. When you show you're listening and you get what they're feeling, it can open the door to a deeper understanding and help smooth things over.

Finding Common Ground

Getting through conflict often means compromising. It's not about one person winning; it's about finding a solution that works for both of you. This could mean coming up with new ideas, looking at things differently, and being open to meeting in the middle. By tackling the problem together, you can find a way forward those respects both of your views and strengthens your relationship.

Learning and Growing Together

Disagreements don't have to be deal-breakers; in fact, they can be just the opposite. Think of them as a classroom for life, where both you and your partner get to learn and evolve, not just on your own, but together. When you bump heads, instead of seeing it as a red flag, try flipping the script and see it as a chance to get stronger as a team. It's like hitting the gym for your relationship – it builds resilience and brings you closer.

Let's break it down: to get through the rough patches, you've got to talk it out, really hear each other, and be ready to meet halfway. It's all about embracing those differences, making sure everyone feels heard, and finding that sweet spot where both of you can say, "Yeah, this works for us." So, when you hit a snag, remember it's all about learning from each other and turning those moments into something that'll make your connection even more awesome.

CHAPTER 4

THE MYTH OF SEX

Navigating the Intricacies of Sexuality in Romantic Bonds

Sexuality is a rich tapestry woven from our physical, emotional, and psychological threads, shaping a crucial part of our human journey. In this discussion, we'll debunk some common myths and explore the truth about sexual dynamics in romantic partnerships, shedding light on how these beliefs influence the way lovers view and engage with each other intimately.

Busting Myths About Bedroom Dynamics

Let's face it, sexuality is shrouded in tall tales and misunderstandings that shape how we think and act in our most intimate moments. Here, we'll tackle some widespread falsehoods about bedroom antics and reveal how busting these myths can lead to a more honest and satisfying sexual rapport between partners.

Myth 1: Perfection is a Must in the Bedroom

The belief that sex should always be flawless and effortless can pile on the pressure, leading to stress and unease for both parties. Sex is a nuanced dance that can fluctuate with each encounter. Couples should understand that it's normal to face occasional hiccups and that these don't reflect the overall health of their bond.

Myth 2: More is Better When It Comes to Sex

Many think that the more often you're intimate, the better your relationship must be. However, it's not about keeping score. The depth and quality of your sexual connection matter far more than the frequency. Strive for a fulfilling and emotionally rich intimacy rather than hitting a certain number of trysts.

Myth 3: Men are Always Ready for Sex

There's a persistent stereotype that men are perpetually keen on sex, while women are more reserved. This not only reinforces damaging gender norms but also ignores the true spectrum of desire across all genders. Both men and women can experience varying levels of desire, and open, stereotype-free communication about needs and wants is crucial.

Myth 4: The Best Sex is Unplanned

Spontaneity can be thrilling, but the notion that top-notch sexual experiences should happen without any forethought isn't always realistic. Partners who talk openly about their likes and boundaries often report greater satisfaction. Planning and communicating can lead to a richer sexual experience that's about more than just impromptu passion.

Myth 5: Sexual Issues Signal a Doomed Relationship

Finally, there's the misconception that any sexual hiccup is a sign of a failing relationship. While sexual chemistry is important, it's not the sole pillar of a partnership. Confronting sexual challenges together, with understanding and a team approach to finding solutions, is key.

In essence, dismantling these myths can pave the way for a more genuine and rewarding sexual connection. By setting aside unrealistic expectations, embracing diverse desires, and prioritizing heartfelt communication, couples can foster a truly satisfying sexual bond.

Building Intimacy Beyond the Physical Realm

True intimacy in a romantic relationship goes much deeper than just physical closeness. Emotional bonds, trust, and mutual understanding are equally essential for a rich and fulfilling partnership. Let's delve into how couples can nurture intimacy that transcends the physical aspect, cultivating a connection that enriches their overall happiness together.

Embracing Emotional Openness

Key to deepening intimacy is the willingness to be emotionally exposed to your partner. Sharing your innermost thoughts and feelings, even when it's tough, can tighten your emotional bond and build trust that extends beyond mere physical attraction.

Making Quality Time a Priority

Spending meaningful time together lays the foundation for closeness. Whether it's enjoying a shared hobby, chatting over dinner, or simply relaxing side by side, regular, quality interactions are vital for nurturing emotional intimacy and strengthening your connection.

Practicing Attentive Listening and Empathy

Good communication is the bedrock of intimacy, and active listening is at its heart. By truly hearing your partner and empathizing with their perspective, you create a safe space for open dialogue, enhancing your emotional bond.

Showing Gratitude and Appreciation

Acknowledging and appreciating your partner can profoundly impact your emotional intimacy. Simple gestures of thanks or deeper expressions of admiration can affirm your partner's value to you and deepen your mutual bond.

Sharing Vulnerabilities and Challenges

While it might be daunting, revealing your insecurities and difficulties to your partner can significantly enhance your emotional callosity. Such honesty allows your partner to see and embrace your true self, fostering a deeper understanding and a more robust, trusting relationship.

Fostering intimacy beyond the physical involves emotional openness, dedicated time together, empathetic listening, heartfelt gratitude, and sharing personal struggles. By focusing on these emotional aspects, couples can forge a deeper, more meaningful connection that amplifies their overall relationship satisfaction and creates a bond that's about more than just physical attraction.

CHAPTER 5

THE MYSTERY OF LOVE

Love is this incredible, deep-seated emotion that's been fascinating to us for ages. It's like this intricate dance of feelings, actions, and experiences that meld our bonds with others and deeply influence our existence. In this section, we're going to dive into the mysterious world of love, looking at its many sides, how it shows up, and what it means for our romantic connections.

Peeling Back the Layers of Love

At its heart, love is something deeply personal and subjective, but it also has this universal importance that crosses cultures and societies. Love isn't just about having warm fuzzies for someone; it's way more complex than that. It can show up as the fiery rush of a new crush or the comfortable vibe of a long-term relationship. It's a mix of happiness, longing, understanding, and dedication, changing and growing as relationships do.

Breaking Down Love's Ingredients

Psychologists have been trying to crack the code of love for a long time, figuring out what makes it tick. Robert Sternberg came up with the idea that love has three big parts:

intimacy, passion, and commitment. Intimacy is all about feeling close and emotionally connected, passion is that spark and intense desire, and commitment is choosing to stick by each other through thick and thin.

Love Through an Evolutionary Lens

From an evolutionary angle, love is pretty important for human survival and making babies. It helps people stick together, take care of each other, and raise kids, ensuring that future generations thrive. Evolutionary psychologists think that things like who we're attracted to and how we act in relationships are influenced by survival tactics honed over time. But even though evolution plays a role, it doesn't capture the full picture of human love.

Culture's Take on Love

Culture shapes love, too. It affects how we see love, how we show it, and how we feel it in our relationships. Different places have their own rules and ideas about love, marriage, and family, which can really change how relationships work and how people experience love. For instance, some cultures value family unity and stability, while others are all about personal happiness and being true to oneself.

The Rough Seas of Love

Love can be the best thing ever, but it's not always smooth sailing. Every relationship hits some rough patches, and getting through them takes patience, understanding, and give-and-take. Plus, life can throw curveballs like work stress or money woes that put extra pressure on our relationships and test how strong our love is.

Embracing Love's Mysteries

No matter how much we try to figure love out, it's still this big, beautiful mystery. It's more than just logic—it's this powerful thing that connects us, inspires us, and gives our lives meaning. While we might not solve the riddle of love, we can keep exploring its wonders, celebrating its magic, and treasuring the deep connections it brings into our lives.

In short, love is this layered, complex emotion that's central to our lives and beyond simple explanations. From where it comes from to how it's expressed, love touches every part of being human. By embracing love's mysteries and its rich variety, we can learn more about ourselves and our relationships, and cultivate a deeper sense of togetherness, compassion, and happiness.

Untangling Love and Attachment

Love and attachment are super intertwined in our relationships, shaping how we connect with others and affecting our emotional health. Next, we're going to look at the ins and outs of love and attachment, their psychological roots, how they start, and what they mean for our romantic lives.

Getting the Scoop on Attachment Theory

Attachment theory, thanks to psychologist John Bowlby, helps us understand why we form the bonds we do, especially the early ones between babies and their caregivers. This theory says that babies build an internal model of relationships from their early interactions, which then guides their future relationship expectations and actions. A secure attachment means feeling safe and comfortable in relationships, while an insecure attachment might make someone anxious or hesitant about getting close.

Attachment's Role in Romance

Attachment theory isn't just for kids; it's super relevant to adult romance, too. It sheds light on how intimacy, loyalty, and communication play out between partners. Studies show that people with secure attachment styles usually have healthier, more satisfying relationships full of trust and support. On the flip side, those with insecure attachment styles might battle with jealousy, fear of being left, and trouble sharing their feelings.

Childhood's Lasting Impact

What happens in childhood can set the stage for how we attach to others as grown-ups. When kids get consistent love, care, and support, they're more likely to develop a secure attachment, which means they'll likely feel safe and trusting in relationships later on. Bad experiences, like neglect or inconsistent care, can lead to insecure attachment, with all the worries and intimacy fears that come with it.

Steering Through Attachment in Romance

Knowing your attachment style and your partner's can make a world of difference in handling the ups and downs of a romantic relationship. This insight can lead to better, more heartfelt communication, tackling deep-seated insecurities, and working together to build a stronger, more loving bond. By creating a relationship that feels safe and secure, couples can grow closer and keep their connection strong over time.

Addressing Insecure Attachment

If you're someone who struggles with insecure attachment, it's crucial to work on breaking those negative cycles of interaction. This means getting to grips with any self-doubt or skewed views on relationships you might hold. It's about becoming more tuned in to your own feelings and treating yourself with kindness. Don't hesitate to lean on friends, family, or even a therapist for a helping hand. Healing from past hurts and moving towards a more secure way of connecting can lay the groundwork for more rewarding and close-knit relationships.

Fostering Deep Connections

Building a deep connection and intimacy in a romantic partnership really boils down to letting your guard down, being real, and showing up emotionally for your partner. Try doing things together that bring you closer, like sharing personal stories, expressing thanks, or simply being there for each other. These acts of love and kindness can bring a new depth to your relationship, making it more enjoyable and meaningful.

Love and attachment are intricate and play a huge role in our relationships and emotional health. By understanding attachment in romance, revisiting our childhood influences, breaking negative cycles, and nurturing closeness with our partners, we can better handle the complexities of love and attachment and create stronger, more fulfilling bonds.

Keeping Love Alive Through Tough Times

Love isn't bulletproof when it comes to the ups and downs of life. But it's often through these tough times that love grows stronger. Here's how couples can keep their love alive and come out on top when faced with life's hurdles.

The Power of Talking It Out

When things get rocky, talking things through is more important than ever. Open and honest chats can help you both air out worries, vent, and figure out what you need from each other. Make it a point to touch base regularly, really listen, and validate each other's feelings. Good communication is the bedrock for facing challenges together, hand in hand.

Growing Stronger Together

Tough times can seem daunting, but tackling them as a duo can make your relationship tougher. Look at challenges as chances to grow and learn together. By drawing on each other's strengths and support, you can come out on the other side more united and resilient.

Staying Flexible

Being able to roll with the punches is key when life throws curveballs at your relationship. When plans change or priorities shift, being flexible can help you both find your way through. Embracing change rather than fighting it can make you both stronger and more adaptable.

Offering Empathy and Support

A little understanding and care can go a long way when you're both under pressure. Showing empathy and support creates a safe space for both of you to be open and connect. By being there for each other, you can face challenges with grace and come out even closer.

Looking After Yourselves

To keep your relationship strong, you've got to look after yourselves, too. When you both take care of your physical, mental, and emotional health, you're in a better place to support each other. So, don't forget to do things that recharge your batteries, whether it's hitting the gym, meditating, or just hanging out with loved ones. Self-care means you'll both be ready to face whatever comes your way.

Celebrating the Wins

Don't forget to high-five each other for the big and small wins, even when times are tough. Acknowledging the good stuff can boost your resilience and keep your connection strong. Whether it's getting through a rough patch or just sharing a giggle, celebrating these moments together can help keep your spirits up through thick and thin.

keeping love alive through challenges is all about communicating, building resilience, staying flexible, being empathetic, taking care of yourselves, and celebrating your wins. By tackling life's obstacles as a team and supporting each other every step of the way, you can navigate the rough with the smooth, strengthening your bond more than ever.

CHAPTER 6

THE PARENT TRAP

The route of life is replete with unanticipated detours and turns. This chapter will discuss how couples can go through life's ups and downs together, fortifying and strengthening their relationship in the process.

Accepting Common Objectives and Dreams
Adopting common aspirations and goals is essential for a relationship to successfully navigate life's path. Having similar goals can give a relationship direction and purpose, whether it's purchasing a home, raising a family, or seeing the world. Couples need to spend time talking about their aspirations and expectations for the future so that they may align their vision and collaborate to achieve their common objectives.

Helping One Another Over Obstacles

There are difficulties in life, and couples will unavoidably run into problems when traveling together. Overcoming obstacles together, be they related to money, health, or job, can improve the relationship between spouses. as things go tough, couples should make an effort to be there for one another by showing compassion, encouraging words, and helpful support as required. Couples can develop resilience and fortitude by overcoming obstacles together, becoming stronger and closer than before.

Sustaining a Robust Trust Foundation

Any successful relationship must be built on trust, and this is especially true while sharing the path of life. Prioritizing honesty, openness, and integrity in their relationships will help couples create a solid foundation of trust that will endure life's ups and downs. In the face of uncertainty, trust enables partners to feel safe and supported, which promotes a sense of security and stability in the partnership.

Speaking Honestly and Openly

As a pair, you must communicate well to navigate life's path together. Open and honest communication about hopes, worries, and concerns should be encouraged between partners without fear of condemnation or backlash. Couples may stay in sync and connected while navigating life's ups and downs together by having open and honest conversations regularly. Couples who encourage candid and open conversation are better able to overcome obstacles and strengthen their bond in the process.

Gratitude in Ordinary Moments

In the face of life's obstacles, couples must find happiness in the small things in life. Finding time to spend together and enjoy one other's company, whether it be during a meal, a stroll, or just cuddling on the couch, can improve the relationship between spouses. Amidst life's busy schedules, couples should emphasize spending quality time together, scheduling time for play, laughing, and relaxation. Couples can develop a sense of thankfulness and appreciation for one another and strengthen their bond by finding delight in the little things in life.

Fostering Adaptability and Flexibility

Because life is unpredictable, couples need to be flexible enough to change course when necessary. Couples who practice flexibility and adaptability are better able to handle life's curveballs with poise and resiliency, coming up with innovative solutions for unforeseen problems and seizing new chances as they present themselves. Knowing that they can weather any storm as a team, couples should approach life's path with an open mind and a readiness to embrace change.

Identifying and Resolving Childhood Influence Patterns
Our early life experiences influence how we view the world, other people, and ourselves. This section will look at how childhood influences can still have an impact on our relationships as adults and how couples can identify and work through these patterns to create happier, more satisfying relationships.

Recognizing Childhood Impacts

We start to assimilate messages about our values and develop relationships to our caregivers the moment we are born. These early encounters meld our attitudes, actions, and interpersonal patterns, which affect how we relate to and engage with people as adults. While negative experiences of abuse, neglect, or inconsistent treatment can cause mistrust, insecurity, and relationship problems, positive experiences of love, support, and validation from childhood can help establish the foundation for healthy and secure relationships as adults.

Recognizing Trends in Adult Partnerships

In mature relationships, patterns from early influences can show up subtly and perhaps unconsciously. These tendencies can show themselves as a need for approval from other people, or an inability to communicate feelings or fears of abandonment. Couples may discover that they are reliving well-known patterns from their early years, such as one partner taking on a caregiver role while the other takes on a more submissive or dependent role. The first step in resolving these tendencies and establishing more positive relational dynamics is identifying them.

Examining Emotional Reactions and Triggers

Events or circumstances known as triggers elicit intense emotional responses based on recollections of the past. For instance, feelings of inadequacy or unworthiness brought on by rejection or neglect experienced as a child may be triggered by a partner's criticism. Couples can learn more about how their early relationships are still influenced by their childhood by investigating these triggers and the underlying feelings they arouse. Couples can react to these triggers more empathetically and understandingly when they are aware of them.

Establishing a Safe and Helpful Environment
Addressing childhood impacts in adult relationships requires establishing a safe and nurturing atmosphere. To facilitate honest and open conversation and to make both partners feel heard, respected, and appreciated, couples should work to establish a safe place. Setting limits on touchy subjects, engaging in empathy and active listening, and providing encouragement and validation for one another's experiences are a few ways to do this. Couples can address underlying difficulties resulting from childhood influences and collaborate to establish healthy marital patterns by providing a safe and supportive environment.

Looking for Expert Assistance

Seeking guidance from a licensed therapist or counsellor may be necessary when addressing patterns resulting from early effects. A qualified expert may assist couples in examining their prior experiences, spotting unhealthy tendencies, and formulating plans for fostering more positive interpersonal dynamics. Couples who are in therapy can process challenging emotions, explore delicate topics, and develop new communication and conflict-resolution skills in a private, safe environment. Couples can strive toward healing and progress together and gain insight into how their childhood influences affect their adult relationships by obtaining professional support.

Dedicated to Developing Oneself and Relationships

 Both spouses must be committed to their own personal and relationship development to address habits resulting from childhood effects. Couples ought to be prepared to examine themselves, accept accountability for their deeds, and make a concerted effort to improve. This could entail putting old habits and beliefs to the test, venturing outside of comfort zones, and trying out novel interpersonal communication techniques. Couples can build a more stable, satisfying, and resilient relationship that respects each other's unique experiences and encourages mutual growth and understanding by making a commitment to personal and relational development.

Overcoming Unhealthy Dynamics in Relationships: Lessons from Parents

Our upbringing has a big impact on the attitudes, behaviors, and beliefs we have about relationships. For better or worse, our parents or other primary caregivers teach us a lot about communication, love, and handling conflict. On the other hand, if those connection patterns were harmful or dysfunctional, they may have an effect on our own adult relationships. It takes self-awareness, reflection, and a commitment to disrupt negative habits to overcome these taught behaviors. We'll look at techniques for resolving toxic relationship dynamics that we picked up from our parents in this section.

Identify Trends

Recognizing the patterns and behaviors that are affecting your own relationships is the first step towards changing problematic relationship dynamics that you have learnt from your parents. Think back on your childhood and the interactions between your parents and yourself. Do you have any consistent communication, conflict-resolution, or emotional display patterns that mimic the actions of your parents? Finding these patterns is crucial to starting change and seeing how they can affect your personal relationships.

Contest Ideas

It is possible for certain attitudes and beliefs regarding love, trust, and intimacy to get internalized when one grows up in a setting where toxic interpersonal dynamics exist. It's critical to examine these ideas and determine whether they are consistent with your personal goals and values. For example, you might have internalized the idea that conflict is inevitable or that showing vulnerability is a sign of weakness if you watched your parents argue or manipulate your emotions on a regular basis. You are able to start developing more positive and empowered relationship dynamics by questioning these assumptions and reinterpreting them.

Seek Therapy or Counselling To overcome toxic relationship patterns that have been ingrained in you by your parents, therapy or counseling can be quite helpful. A licensed therapist can offer a secure and encouraging setting for you to examine your past, spot negative habits, and create more positive interpersonal relationships. You can discover the underlying reasons of your relationship problems and get useful techniques for severing rooted habits and ideas through therapy.

Exercise Self-Compassion

Resolving problematic relationship dynamics is a path that calls for tolerance, forgiveness of oneself, and self-compassion. It's critical to understand that although you have the ability to alter the relationship patterns you inherited from your parents, you are not responsible for them. As you traverse the process of unlearning old behaviors and forming new ones, treat yourself with love and understanding as a way to practice self-compassion. Recognize that it takes time and effort to make changes in yourself and practice patience.

Establish Limits

Establishing boundaries is crucial to preserving wholesome relationships and safeguarding your mental health. Setting boundaries with your partner or other people in your life could be required if you find yourself reverting to the same behavioral patterns that you acquired from your parents. This could be being explicit in expressing your needs and boundaries, standing up for yourself when necessary, and placing self-care and self-respect first.

Develop Positive Communication Skills

Lastly, intentionally developing positive relationship behaviors and abilities is a necessary step in overcoming dysfunctional relationship dynamics that are learned from parents. This could entail studying effective dispute-resolution techniques, honing your empathy and active listening abilities, developing communication skills, and placing a high value on mutual respect and understanding in your relationships. Through deliberate efforts to cultivate these abilities, it is possible to establish connections that are founded on genuineness, confidence, and reciprocity. In conclusion, it takes self-awareness, reflection, and a determination to change to overcome toxic interpersonal dynamics that are learned from parents. Through pattern recognition, belief challenges, therapy or counseling, self-compassion exercises, boundary setting, and the development of healthy relationship skills, you can overcome the impact of your past and build more meaningful relationships as an adult.

Making Your Blueprint for a Healthy Relationship

We have the ability to create our own blueprint for a successful relationship, even though our upbringing may have an impact on how we view relationships. Relationships that reflect our genuine selves can be shaped by thinking back on the past, establishing principles, and making plans. We will look at how to make a customized relationship blueprint in this part.

Think Back on the Past

Start by thinking back on your previous relationship experiences, both good and bad. Think on the patterns, dynamics, and communication styles you saw in your family and past relationships. Decide which traits you want to imitate and which ones you want to stay away from. This self-reflection offers insightful information about your values and desired connections.

Establish Your Principles

Next, list your priorities and guiding principles for relationships. What attributes are you looking for in a mate? Which actions are you unwilling to compromise on? Your values act as a set of guidelines for how you wish to behave and be handled in a romantic setting. Trust, communication, honesty, and respect are a few examples of values.

Declare Your Goals

 Clearly define the kind of relationship you wish to build. Imagine being in a relationship that reflects your ideals and promotes your personal development and well-being. Think about things like communication, intimacy, emotional connection, and common objectives. You can maintain focus on the aspects of your relationships that are most important to you by setting intentions.

Share Boundaries

Setting limits is necessary to keep relationships in good shape. Make sure your partner understands your boundaries and that you respect theirs as well. In a relationship, boundaries help establish what is appropriate and inappropriate behavior and foster a feeling of security and trust. Review limits frequently and make any adjustments to make sure they reflect your values and comfort zone.

Engage in Effective Communication

Healthy relationships are built on effective communication. Develop polite, sincere, and open lines of communication with your spouse. To promote comprehension and connection, engage in active listening, empathy, and validation practices. Be open to hearing your partner's point of view and prepared to communicate your needs, wants, and concerns in an aggressive and transparent manner.

Prioritize Self-Care

Self-care is essential for nurturing healthy relationships. Take care of your physical, emotional, and mental well-being by prioritizing activities that recharge and replenish you. Set aside time for self-reflection, hobbies, and activities that bring you joy and fulfillment. Remember that taking care of yourself allows you to show up as your best self in your relationships.

Accept Development and Adaptability

Relationships change over time, therefore it's critical to welcome development and adaptability. Allow yourself to grow and learn with your companion. Acknowledge that obstacles and disagreements present chances for development and closer relationships. Disagreements should be approached with curiosity and a desire to find win-win solutions.

Honour accomplishments

No matter how tiny, acknowledge and celebrate your relationship's accomplishments. Recognize and value the efforts you and your partner put out to strengthen your bond and get through challenges as a team. Thank each other for the love, support, and happiness you provide to each other's life.

CONCLUSION

As you create your blueprint for a healthy relationship, you are setting out on a path of personal growth and self-discovery. Relationships that are authentic to you are a result of your reflections on the past, your definition of values, and your intentional setting. By establishing healthy boundaries, communicating clearly, and placing self-care first, you've given yourself the capacity to overcome obstacles and foster satisfying relationships.

Recall that building wholesome connections takes time, effort, and intentionality. Accept the chances for development and education that come with every connection. No matter how tiny, acknowledge and appreciate your accomplishments, and respond to losses with fortitude and empathy.

Stay loyal to who you are and what you stand for as you proceed on your journey. Make sure the people in your life provide you joy and encouragement, and be prepared to do the same for your spouse. You can build relationships that give you joy, fulfillment, and long-lasting happiness if you practice mindfulness, empathy, and a growth-oriented mindset.

Let's build partnerships that truly represent your best self and your ideal self. May love, compassion, and limitless opportunities abound on your path.

Dear Reader,

Thank you for choosing to read this book. I hope you found the insights and strategies within these pages helpful and empowering on your journey to enhanced communication and confidence.

Your thoughts and feedback are incredibly valuable to me. Reviews not only help other readers discover this book but also allow me to understand how my work resonates with you and where I can continue to improve.

 If you enjoyed this book or found it beneficial, I would greatly appreciate it if you could take a few moments to leave a review on Amazon or any of your preferred platforms. Your honest feedback will help others in similar situations find the support and guidance they need.

Thank you for being a part of this journey. Your support means the world to me.

Warm regards,

Paul E. Kirsch

www.ingramcontent.com/pod-product-compliance
Lightning Source LLC
Chambersburg PA
CBHW051852250726
48659CB00006B/2172